SEAHORSE

LIFE CYCLES

Words that look like **this** can be found in the glossary on page 24.

BookLife
PUBLISHING

©2018
BookLife Publishing
King's Lynn
Norfolk PE30 4LS

Printed in Malaysia.

A catalogue record for this book is available from the British Library.

ISBN: 978-1-78637-380-9

Written by:
Madeline Tyler

Edited by:
Kirsty Holmes

Designed by:
Danielle Rippengill

CONTENTS

WHAT IS A LIFE CYCLE?

All animals, plants and humans go through different stages oftheir life as they grow and change. This is called a life cycle.

Human Life Cycle

WHAT IS A SEAHORSE?

A seahorse is a type of fish. They live in oceans all over the world. They are called seahorses because their heads look like horses' heads.

COURTSHIP

When a female seahorse is trying to find a **mate**, she travels to the male's **territory**. The seahorses change colour, twist their tails together and dance with each other. This is called courtship.

The dance can sometimes last for an hour.

At the end of the dance, the female seahorse puts her eggs inside the male seahorse's special egg pouch, called a brood pouch.

EGGS

After she puts her eggs inside the male's pouch, the male **fertilises** them. The female then starts preparing the next set of eggs straight away.

The female returns to her territory to prepare her eggs.

Smaller seahorses can only carry around 150 eggs.

Seahorses can have up to 1,500 eggs. The eggs are very small so that they can all fit inside the male's pouch.

PREGNANCY

The male seahorse keeps all of the eggs safe for around four weeks. The brood pouch gives the eggs lots of **nutrients** and helps them grow healthy and strong.

Seahorses are very unusual. They are one of the only animals where the male is pregnant and not the female.

FRY

Baby seahorses are called fry. Fry are born after around one month. They are very small and look like mini adult seahorses.

Fry are very **independent**.

As soon as fry are born, they swim away from their father. The fry have to find their own food and protect themselves from **predators**.

SEAHORSES

Fry need to eat lots of food to grow into **juveniles**. Seahorses eat shrimp and baby fish, and fry have to eat up to 3,000 pieces of food every day.

Fry become adults after around six months. Only around one fry out of every 1,000 survives to become an adult. Lots of fry are killed by predators.

TYPES OF SEAHORSES

There are over 40 different **species** of seahorse. Barbigant's pygmy seahorse is a small species and has very good **camouflage** to help it hide from predators.

The spiny seahorse is sometimes called the thorny seahorse. Spiny seahorses can grow up to 17 centimetres (cm) long. They are usually found 15 metres underwater.

SEAHORSE FACTS

Seahorses' tails are very useful. They use them to hold onto plants and coral, or sometimes onto another seahorse. This stops them from getting swept away by the sea.

Seahorses are not very good swimmers. They are very slow and can only swim up to 150 cm every hour.

WORLD RECORD BREAKERS

Biggest Seahorse Caught

The biggest seahorse ever caught in the wild was 34 cm long. It was a spiny seahorse and was caught by Michael Bailey in Dorset, England.

Michael Bailey released the seahorse back into the sea after he took a photograph.

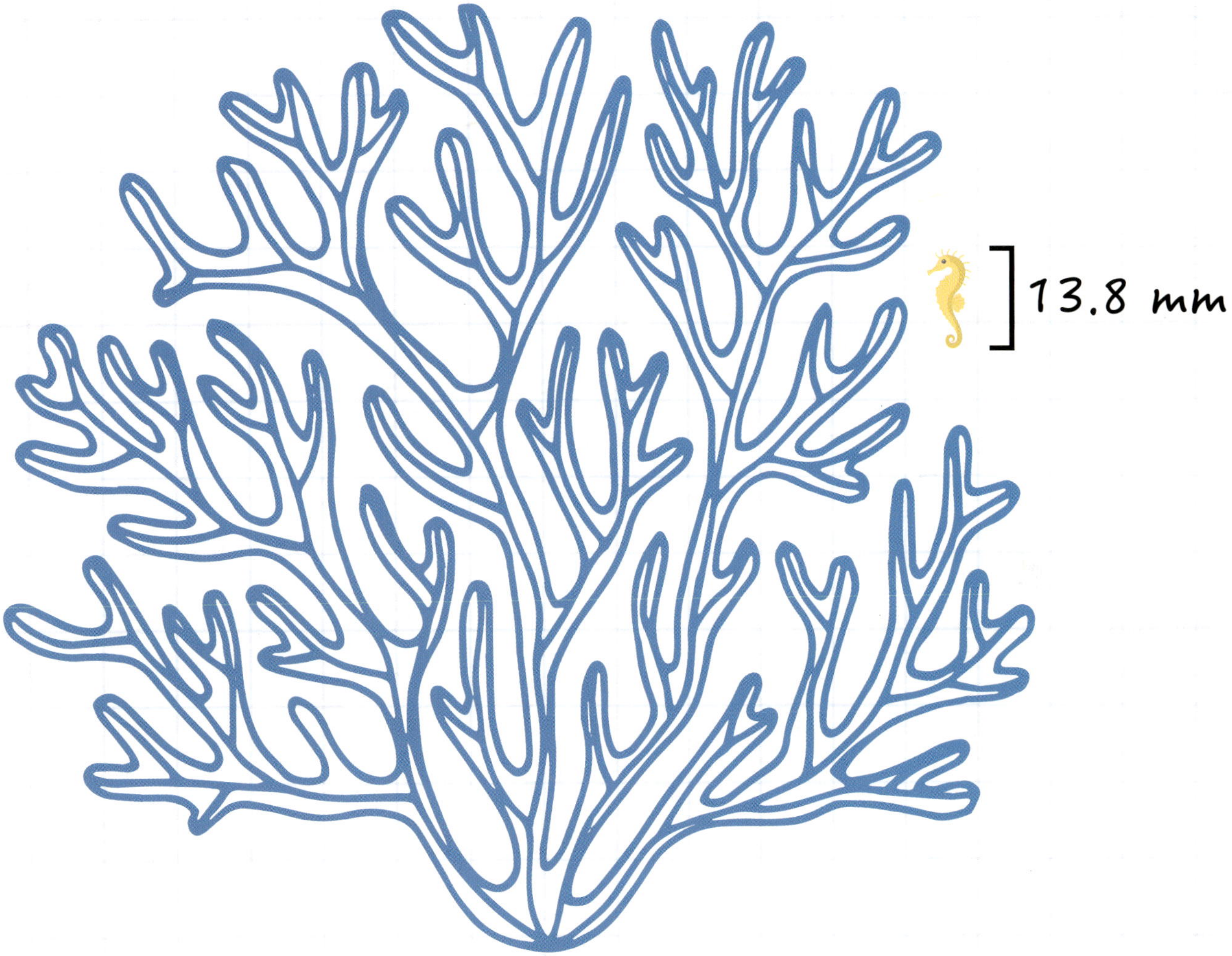

World's Smallest Seahorse

The smallest seahorse in the world is the Satomi's pygmy seahorse. It is only 13.8 millimetres (mm) long.

LIFE CYCLE OF A SEAHORSE

1. Seahorses find a mate by dancing with each other.

2. The female seahorse puts her eggs into the male seahorse's brood pouch. She starts to get her next eggs ready.

3. After around four weeks, the eggs hatch inside the pouch. The male gives birth to the fry.

4. The fry have to look after themselves. They become adults after six months.

GET EXPLORING!

Would you like to learn more about seahorses and their life cycles? See if you can visit a local **aquarium** to see some real seahorses for yourself!

GLOSSARY

aquarium a place containing tanks of many different sea creatures
camouflage traits that allow an animal to hide itself in a habitat
fertilises to cause an egg to develop into a new living thing
independent not needing help or support of another
juveniles young and not grown-up yet
mate a partner (of the same species) who an animal chooses to produce young with
nutrients natural substances that plants and animals need to grow and stay healthy
predators animals that hunt other animals for food
pregnant when a mother develops a baby inside of her
released set free
species a group of very similar animals or plants that are capable of producing young together
territory an area that an animal defends from other animals

INDEX

PHOTO CREDITS

All images are courtesy of Shutterstock.com, unless otherwise specified. With thanks to Getty Images, Thinkstock Photo and iStockphoto. Frontcover – Nantawat Chotsuwan. 1 – Nantawat Chotsuwan. 2 – Choi Ka Kwan. 3 – creativemarc, Rich Carey. 4 – Africa Studio, Daxiao Productions, Maksim Shmeljov. 5 – Frolova_Elena. 6 – Steven L. Gordon. 7 – icedmocha. 8 – Kjeld Friis. 9 – Rich Carey. 10 – Ritu Manoj Jethani. 11 – Hiso. 12 – Nazir Amin. 13 – Choi Ka Kwan. 14 – Fiona Ayerst. 15 – GUDKOV ANDREY. 16 – Ethan Daniels. 17 – Kristina Vackova. 18 – megastocker. 19 – GOLFX. 20 – NotionPic. 21 – Creative Stall, Egor Shilov. 22 – creativemarc, Hiso, Andrea Izzotti, GOLFX. 23 – FamVeld.